My Hands

by Aliki

Revised Edition

Thomas Y. Crowell   New York

for Esther Hautzig

LET'S READ-AND-FIND-OUT BOOK CLUB EDITION

The *Let's-Read-and-Find-Out Science Book* series was originated by Dr. Franklyn M. Branley, Astronomer Emeritus and former Chairman of the American Museum–Hayden Planetarium, and was formerly co-edited by him and Dr. Roma Gans, Professor Emeritus of Childhood Education, Teachers College, Columbia University.

Let's-Read-and-Find-Out Science Book is a registered trademark of Harper & Row, Publishers, Inc.

MY HANDS
Printed in the United States of America.
1   2   3   4   5   6   7   8   9   10
Revised Edition

Library of Congress Cataloging-in-Publication Data
Aliki.
  My hands / by Aliki. — Rev. ed.
    p.   cm. — (Let's-read-and-find-out science book)
  Summary: Describes the parts of the hand and all the things our hands help us to do.
  ISBN 0-690-04878-5 : $. — ISBN 0-690-04880-7 (lib. bdg.) : $
  1. Hand—Anatomy—Juvenile literature. [1. Hand.] I. Title.
II. Series.
QM548.A45   1990b   89-49158
612'.97—dc20   CIP
                                                       AC

My Hands

Peek-a-boo!
Do you ever play finger games?

Do you ever count on your fingers?

If you do, you know what I know.
I have two hands.

I have a left hand

and a right hand.

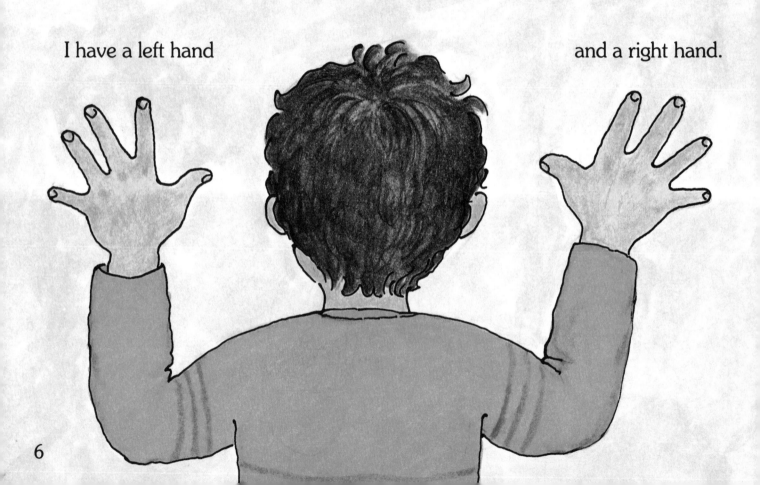

Each hand has five fingers.
Each finger has a name.
The names are:

Index   Middle

Ring

Thumb   Little

The thumb is the thickest finger.

The index finger is the pointer.

The middle finger is the longest finger.

The ring finger holds the rings.

The little finger is the smallest of all.
Some people call it the "Pinky."

9

Each finger has a nail.

The nail protects the finger.

My fingernails help me pick up little things.

I put my hands together.
The fingers of my right hand
touch the same fingers of my left hand.

Now I stretch my fingers.

Two are different from all the others.

My thumbs!

They point side to side when the others point up and down.

They point up and down
when the others point side to side.

My thumb can touch any of my other fingers.

I use my thumb and fingers to hold and grasp things.
Try to hold a pencil without using your thumb.

Try to button a button without using your thumb.
Try to snap your fingers without your thumb.
It is not easy.
We use our thumbs all the time.

This is the palm of my hand.
I hold things in my palms.

I use my palms to make snowballs.

I use my palms to pat, to clap, and to roll clay.

My fingertips are sensitive.
They tell me if I touch something

hot

cold

smooth

rough

or prickly.

I am left-handed.
Some people are right-handed.
Some people are ambidextrous!
They can use both hands for doing things.

My hands are covered with smooth skin.

Inside, there are many bones.

I can feel my knuckles.

If I look hard, I can see pale-blue veins.

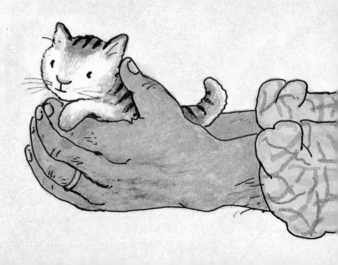

Daddy's hands are different from mine.
They are big and rough and bony.

Mother's hands are soft...

21

…and Grandpa's are veined and wrinkled.
Baby sister's hands will grow to be as big as mine.
My hands will grow, too.

But I can do many things with my hands right now.
I use them to push and to pull,

to cut and to build.

23

I use my hands to dig or tickle or eat,

to scratch or swat or hammer.

I use my hands to make music and to play games.
Some people talk with their hands.
Deaf people use sign language.

I use my hands on sunny days

on rainy days

even on cold days.

On all days my hands help me have good manners.
I cover every cough and sneeze and yawn.

Some people use their hands to help them shout

or to say *shhhhh*.

I use mine to say hello and good-bye.

For work or play,
people use their hands,
and you do, too.

Put your hands on your head.
See how long you can keep them there
without needing them.

See? How else could you have turned the page?